Western Oklahoma

Publication of this work was made possible

by a generous contribution from

GHK Gas Corporation

A Photographic Essay

Western Oklahoma

Photographs by Daisy Decazes
Text by William S. Banowsky

UNIVERSITY OF OKLAHOMA PRESS : NORMAN

Library of Congress Cataloging in Publication
Data

Decazes, Daisy, 1955–
    Western Oklahoma.

    1. Oklahoma—Description and travel—1981–
—Views. I. Banowsky, William Slater. II. Title.
F695.D4   976.6   82–2670
                    AACR2

Acknowledgments

I would like to acknowledge the assistance given to
me by Monte and Floyd Truman, Marty Jennings, Jim
Ikard, Manuel and Teresa Da Silva, Scott Woodward,
Edwin Kolb, Marilyn Myers, Bettye Ames, Bill Rob-
bins, Suzan Mears, Walter Merrick, and Ladd Hitch.

The photographs in this book are dedicated to Rob-
ert A. Hefner III and to Bill Jennings, who believe that
Western Oklahoma holds great spirit, energy, and future, and to my parents.

Daisy Decazes

Introduction

By William S. Banowsky

Western Oklahoma demands heroes.

Through the years have come the nomadic hunters, gold-seeking conquistadors, rebellious Plains Indians, trail-blazing cattlemen, land-hungry settlers, and wild-cat oilmen. It took guts, heartache, and bloodshed to tame this country. The terse truism applies: The cowards did not come; the weaklings never made it; only the strong survived.

As a native southwesterner, I have known the pioneers' stories since childhood. But French-born Daisy Decazes approached this rugged and beautiful land with utter freshness. Through her vision the essence of Western Oklahoma is captured.

Love of the land wears different faces. Long ago the Plains Apaches followed the great buffalo herds into Western Oklahoma, and the Wichitas and Caddos farmed near the Red and the Arkansas rivers. The land, trees, streams, wind, rain, and sun—these forces comprised a whole that lived in harmony. The idea of exploiting the land never occurred to the Indians. It belonged to everybody.

As every Oklahoma schoolchild knows, the Five Civilized Tribes endured the heartbreak and suffering of their Trail of Tears to Indian Territory between 1812 and 1842. Originally their writ ran to Oklahoma's present western boundary, excluding the Panhandle, which did not become United States territory until 1850. Between 1830 and 1855, Western Oklahoma belonged to the Cherokees in the north, the Creeks and Seminoles in the center, and the Choctaws and Chickasaws in the south. In reality, however, almost all the settlements and ranches of the Five Civilized Tribes were in Eastern Oklahoma. Western Oklahoma remained the province of the Plains Apaches, the Wichitas, the Caddos, the Comanches, the Kiowas, and the Kiowa-Apaches. The hunting tribes killed buffalo, resisted the incursion of settlers, and raided American settlements in Texas, but, increasingly, they found their territory ever smaller and their access to buffalo restricted.

By the 1880s the Indians were struggling to keep their country. Cattlemen supported their efforts, but the lush grasses attracted the covetous attention of railroad and mercantile interests, who saw the underdeveloped country as a profit source. They encouraged men known as "Boomers" to promote opening of the Indian lands.

The sun shone brilliantly on Monday, April 22, 1889. Homeseekers, some 50,000 of them, waited on the four borders of the Oklahoma District. At noon bugles blew, a cannon roared, and the Run of 1889 began. Homeseekers on horseback, in carriages, clinging to the sides of special trains, and on foot rushed into the open country. Some, known derisively as Sooners, crept early onto the land, hid, and then stepped out shortly after noon to stake claims. By nightfall almost every claim was taken. Campfires gleamed on the prairie, marking the tent cities at Guthrie and Oklahoma City.

In 1890, Congress passed the Oklahoma Organic Act, which organized Oklahoma Territory and provided for the addition to it of other portions of Indian Territory as they were settled. It also attached the Panhandle—No Man's Land—to Oklahoma Territory. Runs, lotteries, and auctions opened the rest of Western Oklahoma, and the United States Supreme Court added Greer County in an 1896 decision.

Early-day settlers needed will and determination to survive. They came mostly from Kansas, Missouri, Texas, Illinois, Iowa, and Indiana, making their first homes in tents, covered wagons, dugouts, and soddies. The remnants of some soddies still stand. They dripped water after a rain. Centipedes rustled, and snakes slithered inside, seeking warmth. Smoky kerosene lanterns gave the only light.

The settlers knew hunger and loneliness and sometimes fear. Then, worst of all, the land turned on them. The 1890s began with a devastating drought that lasted until rains finally came in the fall and winter of 1895–96. The summer of 1896 brought a good wheat crop; the summer of 1897, a bumper crop. Wheat became profitable. Farmers planted more and more of it, and cotton flourished in the south.

In 1907, Oklahoma Territory and Indian Territory were joined as the state of Oklahoma, a land that demanded the utmost from its people and returned in kind: fabulous crops and soon rich oil fields.

Unfortunately, the white settlers destroyed as they built, ravaging within a few years the complex ecology of the Plains. They replaced thick-rooted grasses with wheat and churned the light, rich soils to exhaustion. Nothing held the soil. In dry times it blew away. In wet times it washed away. By 1900 erosion had scarred much of Oklahoma into a lifeless pattern of gullies and sand-scrubbed wastes. By 1939 one-fourth of the state's soil had been lost to production through erosion.

The day of reckoning came in the 1930s. A major drought shriveled the land. Dust hung in the northwest, huge clouds that moved with the wind, sweeping across the country and into towns. It blew everywhere, clogging the air, blanketing the sky with a dull-orange haze. Sometimes the roads in Western Oklahoma were closed because drivers could not see. Sometimes breathing was almost impossible.

In 1935 a farm wife, Caroline A. Henderson, of Shelton, in the Panhandle, described the Dust Bowl to Henry Wallace, United States secretary of agriculture. She wrote: "There are days when for hours we cannot see the windmill 50 feet from the kitchen door. There are days when for briefer periods we cannot distinguish the windows from the solid wall because of the solid blackness from the raging storm. Only in some Inferno-like dream could anyone visualize the terrifying lurid red light overspreading the sky when portions of Texas are 'on the air.' This wind-driven dust, fine as the finest flour, penetrates wherever air can go."

The land turned to powder, dust that blew and dust that rippled in dunes against abandoned farmhouses and barns. Nature conspired with the economic plague of the Great Depression to devastate the region. In 1933 the price of live cattle dropped to four cents a pound. Banks foreclosed on mortgages. Stores closed. Few had any money, and those who did could not plant seed in a withered land. Defeated Oklahomans, about 220,000 of them, piled their goods atop rickety cars and drove west on Highway 66, looking for work, anywhere, everywhere.

Many left. Others stayed, finding the will and tenacity and luck—for life needs luck too—to survive. Those who persevered planted thousands of trees, building shelterbelts across the open plains. They dammed creeks and gullies to halt erosion. They cut terraces on hillsides and plowed crosswind in the open fields. They planted soil-holding grasses, turning millions of parched acres into fertile earth again. The land revived. Today Oklahoma crops feed the world, and agriculture yields over $1 billion annually to the state's economy. Wheat earns Oklahomans $665 million a year, cotton $100 million, and cattle $2 billion. The inventory value of Oklahoma horses is estimated at $568 million.

Hardship, risk, and struggle forged the character of Western Oklahomans. Settlers survived because they recognized that life is change. They piled their goods onto wagons and took their families out into a lonely country where coyotes howled at night.

One grand example of survival is the Hitch Ranch, near Guymon. Begun by James K. Hitch in the 1890s with 200 head of cattle, it was expanded into a wheat and cattle empire by his son, Henry C. Hitch. Today it is an agribusiness run by the Hitch family on a highly mechanized ranch with an airplane, a fleet of cars, and an office in Guymon, which has a small TV monitor spliced into the Chicago futures market.

Perhaps the most dramatic and pervasive change in the history of Western Oklahoma is occurring now, a change so profound that it will mark a watershed not only for Oklahoma but for the entire nation.

A new breed of hero strides the land, the deep-gas driller in the Anadarko Basin. Both major oil companies and independent operators are heavily involved.

The Anadarko Basin curves like a thick comet's tail from just north of Lawton into the Texas Panhandle. From Lawton to Elk City ancient sands trap gas reserves at depths to 50,000 feet, dipped there 350 million years ago in a violent volcanic wrench.

Deep-gas drilling demands prodigious technology. A single well can cost $10 million. Drillers cope with blowout-threatening pressures that build up to 20,000 pounds per square inch. Temperatures range up to 400 degrees Fahrenheit.

The burst of drilling in the basin is linked directly to passage of the Natural Gas Policy Act of 1978, which decontrolled all new gas produced from below 15,000 feet. Before the act, most deep gas sold for about 22 cents per thousand cubic feet. Decontrolled, the new deep gas sells for much more. Accordingly, the Anadarko Basin explodes with rigs, more activity than has ever before been seen in Oklahoma, even in its young black-gold heyday.

The Anadarko Basin is the most meteoric chapter in Oklahoma's long romance with oil and gas. In 1981 more than 550 deep-gas wells were drilling or completing there. But it is the same old story. Just as the pioneers and cattlemen and farmers risked the present to gain the future, so do the deep-gas drillers. Instead of standing hip-deep in dust, they stand hip-deep in debt, gambling on their skill and expertise and instinct to find and bring up billions of cubic feet of gas, enriching themselves, their state, and their country. These drillers believe they have found the answer to America's energy crisis. They believe it. They are proving it.

This is Western Oklahoma.

The Photographs

Prairie aristocrat

Wickham Ranch, north of Elk City

Heading home

Wickham Ranch

The furrowed land

Farm near Clinton

Vestiges of ancient days

Dinosaur tracks, Black Mesa Park

Building with what they had

Dugout remains, Hitch Ranch, near Guymon

Original settler

Prairie Dog, Wichita Mountains

Majestic morning

Antelope Hills

Sweet August harvest

Watermelon Festival, Rush Springs

Prairie oasis

Reydon, north of Sayre

Early risers

Roll, north of Cheyenne

Main Street

Eighty-niners Day, Guthrie

Panhandle faces

"Santa Fe Trail Daze" parade, Boise City

Waiting for the bus

Kenton, in the Oklahoma Panhandle

Sanctuary

Elk City

We gather together

Church of Christ, Crawford

Blue denim Monday

Woodward County

Morning after the dance

Freedom, in Woods County

Prairie gothic

Anadarko

Coyote kill

Crawford Ranch, north of Cheyenne

Wichita bugler

Elk, Wichita Mountains

Black Mesa beauties

Black Mesa Park

Abandoned

Near Freedom

Moved to town

North of Elk City

Autumn on the home place

Near Kenton

Drift fence

Hitch Ranch

Chapparal country

Atop Black Mesa, looking toward Colorado

Morning haze

Between Freedom and Alabaster Caverns

Cactus in the storm

Black Mesa Park

The burnished hills

Glass Mountains, southwest of Alva

Lone tree

South of Freedom

Country calm

Near Geary

Abundance for winter

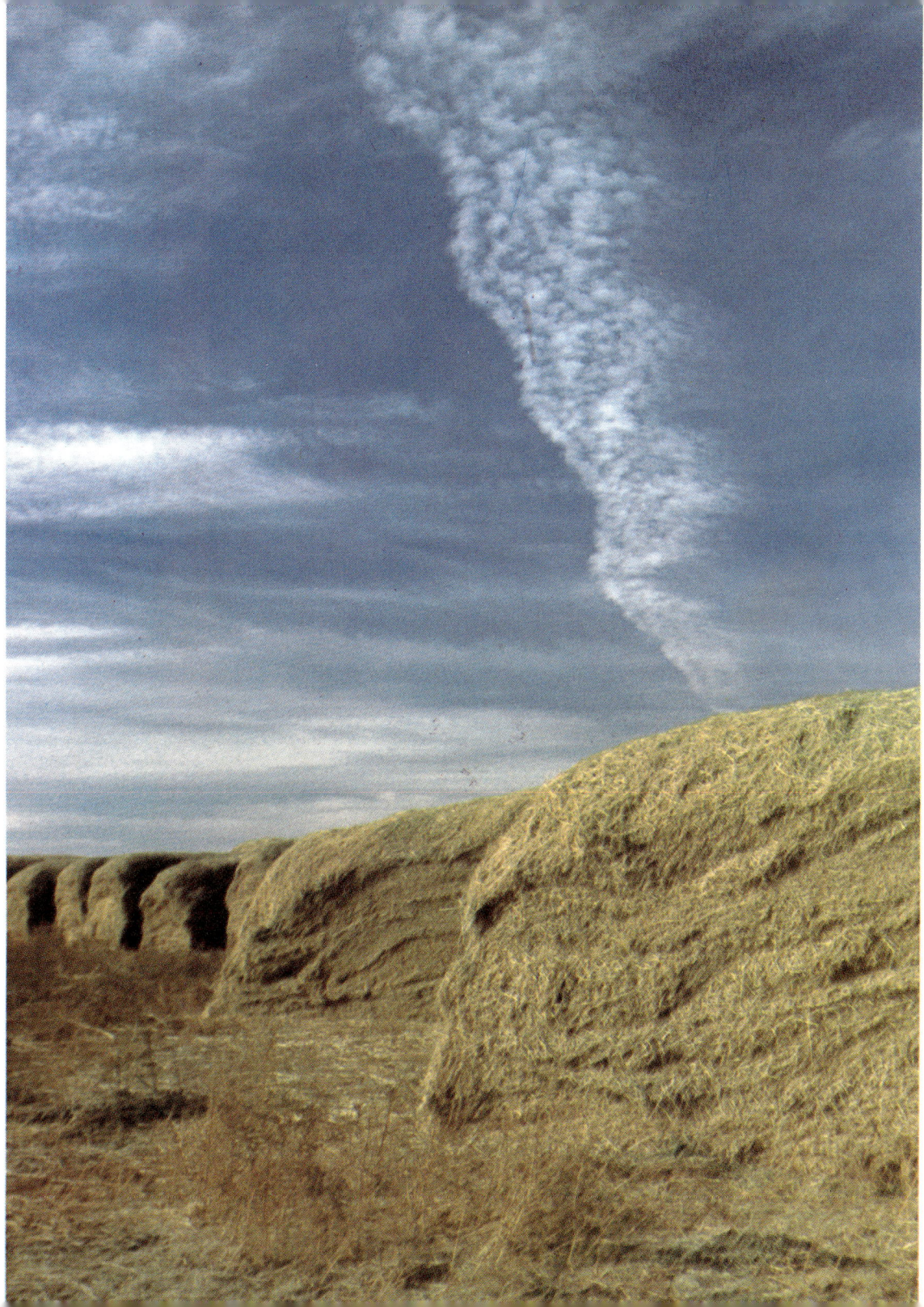

Haystacks, Hitch Ranch

Saturday afternoon

Watermelon Festival, Rush Springs

Riding into town

Freedom

Breaking the heat

Freedom

Out of chute 1

Rodeo, Oklahoma City

Bring on the clowns

Rodeo, Guthrie

Tough ride

Rodeo, Oklahoma City

Telling a friend

Anadarko

At the races

Anadarko

Kiowa campground

Carnegie

Win, place, and show

Anadarko

The night dancers

Geary

Shortgrass country

North of Elk City

Harvest eve

Near Clinton

Moon Lark

Big money winner, Merrick 14 Ranch, Sayre

Bins of plenty

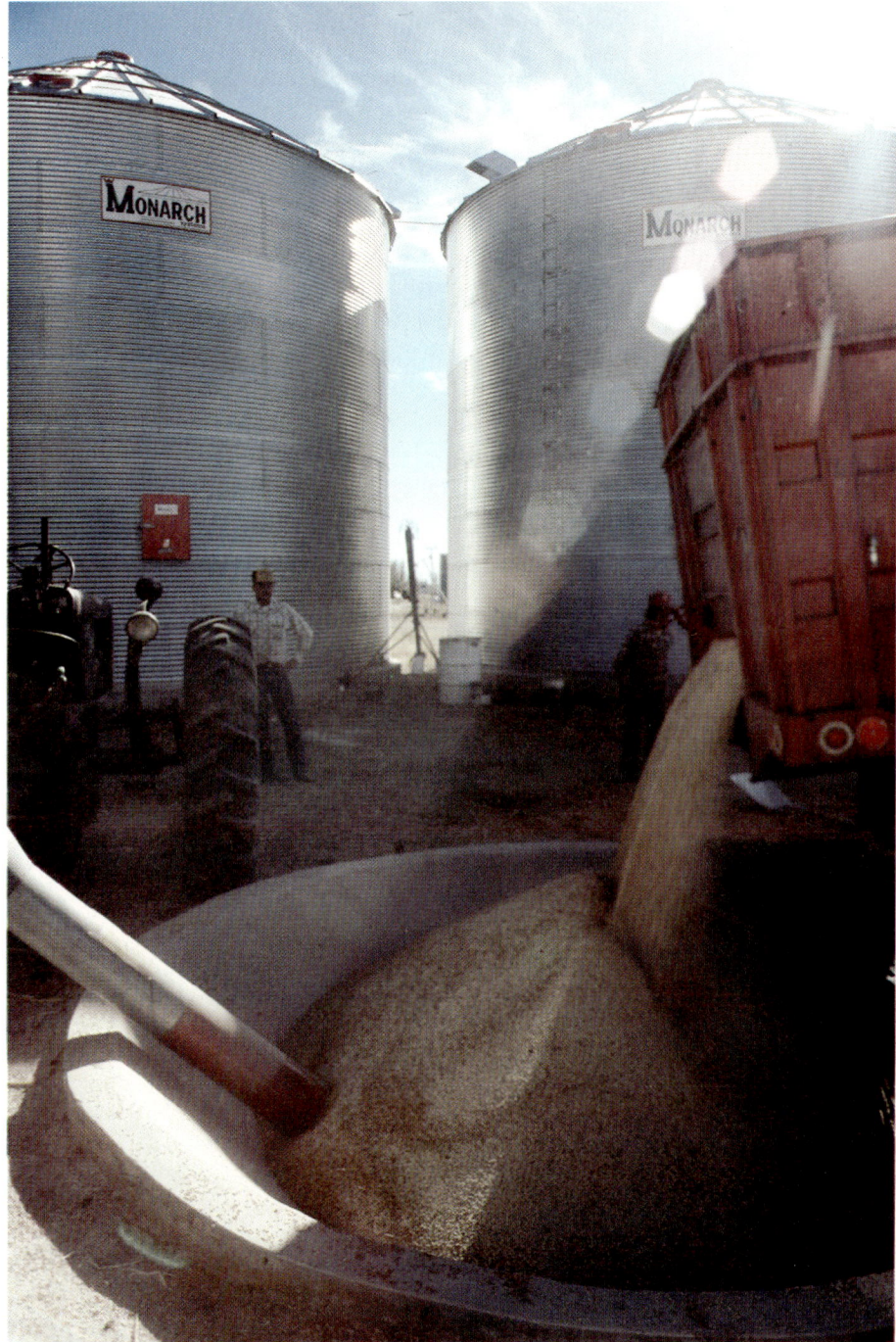

Milo harvest, Boise City

The greening of summer

Irrigation, Hitch Ranch

Fields of furrows

Northwest of Boise City

Cottonfields

West of Clinton

Chuckwagon

Near Boise City

Indian summer

Near Crawford

Sweet tooth

Vitamin-enriched molasses, Crawford Ranch

No more cattle drives

Feedlot, Cherokee

The silver road

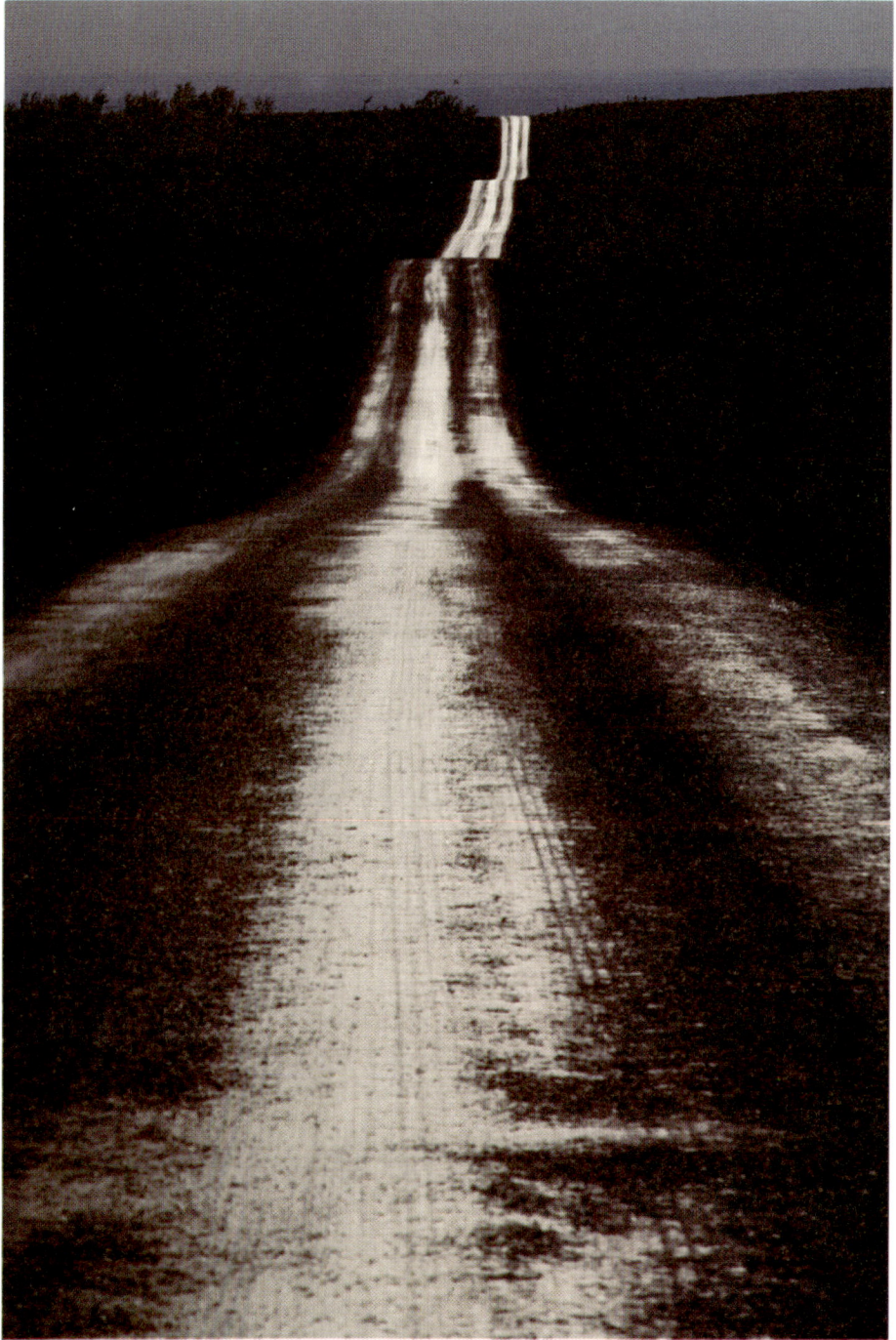

North of Elk City

Heading for town

North to Elk City

Patrolling the land

Rangers, Wichita Wildlife Refuge

Sun storm

Black Mesa Park

Moonrise

Over Lake Hefner, Oklahoma City

Independence Day

Fort Sill

Salute to the nation

Fort Sill

Lest we forget

Fort Sill

End of the shift

1-18 Dugger, GHK deep-gas well, Custer County

Oklahoma nightscape

1-18 Dugger

Tripping out

Changing the pipe, 1-2 Harrell, GHK deep-gas well, Washita County

Rig up to run casing

1-2 Harrell

Fueling America

Champlin Refinery, Enid

Windbreak

Black Mesa Park

Belonging

Near Boise City

Red sky

On the road to Guymon

New day

North of Sayre

Last light of day

Wichita Mountains

Prairie relic

Wichita Mountains

Longhorn roundup

Wichita Mountains

Remembering yesterday

"Santa Fe Trail Daze," Boise City

Designed by Bill Cason, *Western Oklahoma* was composed by the University of Oklahoma Press in 9-, 12-, and 14-point Olympus, with handset Eras Bold used for the display type. Color separations and presswork were done by Christian Board of Publication on 100 # Warren's Patina. Binding was done by the Becktold Company.